RUGBY UNION

PLAY THE GAME

RUGBY UNION

IAN MORRISON

BLANDFORD

First published in Great Britain in 1989. Revised
in 1993 by Blandford, Villiers House,
41–47 Strand, London WC2N 5JE
A Cassell Imprint

Reprinted 1993, 1994

Designed by Anita Ruddell

Illustrated by Bob Williams

Text set in Helvetica
by Hourds Typographica, Stafford, England
Printed and bound in Great Britain by
The Bath Press, Avon

British Library Cataloguing in Publication Data
Morrison, Ian, 1947–
    Play the game rugby union.
    1. Rugby Union football
    I. Title
    796.33'3

ISBN 0-7137-2418-8

Acknowledgments

The author and publishers would like to
thank Colorsport for supplying all the
photographs reproduced in this book.

Front cover: **Australia's David Campese runs clear of Barbarian defence. His ability
to change direction but maintain pace makes him difficult to tackle.**

Frontispiece: **A master kicker. With field position and points so dependant on a
reliable kicker, Australia have been well served by Michael Lynagh whose touch
kicks, drop goals, penalties and conversions have often been the difference between
them and their opponents.**

CONTENTS

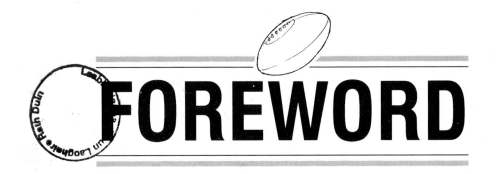

FOREWORD

Rugby Union has over the last decade emerged onto the International Sporting Arena. It is played throughout the world and the recent innovation of two World Cup competitions has seen this interest mushroom. Five years ago New Zealand donned the mantle of World Champions in 1987 achieving the highest standards of fitness, skill and style of play that had ever been witnessed.

By the time the second World Cup was staged at Twickenham in 1991 Australia had emerged as the champions. They along with England had learnt the lessons of the first tournament and set out to successfully emulate the New Zealand approach. You must never stand still in this world otherwise you will get overtaken!

I was first introduced to rugby union as a schoolboy and have never looked back. The schools do an enormous amount to promote the game amongst the young but increasingly the burden is falling upon the rugby clubs themselves to find, introduce the players to and then keep them interested in the game. Small sided games with limited contact concentrating on the skill aspects of the game are aimed at opening up the game to as many young people as possible of all shapes and sizes.

This book is an ideal resource for those involved in wanting to find out more detail about the game. It offers a nuts and bolts approach enabling a newcomer to get a meaningful flavour of what this game of physical chess is all about. It illustrates the history and development of the game and goes on to describe the terminology used and the equipment required. This section also will be very useful for the unindoctrinated as will the section on the laws of the game. The rules clinic section is particularly helpful in this complex area of the game.

Essentially rugby football requires the application of some simple basic technique. The final chapter gives adequate advice on all of these with additional advice for players in their various positions. All in all the book provides a comprehensive over-view of the game at a level suitable to all but the top echelons of the game. Reading this book won't guarantee to make you a better player, coach or spectator but it will certainly help if you are prepared to make use of the information it offers. **Dudley Wood**
Secretary, Rugby Football Union

HISTORY &
DEVELOPMENT OF
RUGBY UNION

Rugby Union is a truly international game, played in countries as diverse as Andorra and Zimbabwe. But it was in England in 1823 that the game was born . . . or so the story goes.

The popular belief has it that one William Webb Ellis was responsible for giving us Rugby football. Historians over the years have tried to disprove this claim but have not been all that successful.

Ellis's contribution was simple. Whilst playing the round-ball version of football that we know today as soccer, he picked up the ball and ran with it. This incident happened during a match at Rugby School and, as many different forms of football rules existed in those days, it was decided that Ellis's version of the game, which involved picking up the ball, should be called Rugby football. Ellis is, therefore, acknowledged as the 'father of the handling game'.

The new game spread quickly, particularly amongst the public schools and universities. Twenty-three years after Ellis's historic run there was a need to formulate the first standardized set of rules, and these were drawn up at Rugby School in 1846. Two years later the Cambridge Rules were drawn

up, and these formed the basis of the Association game, when the Football Association was set up in 1863.

Although footballs in the mid-nineteenth century were far from round, it was not until 1851 that a 'Rugby School football' was seen. It was more oval than the normal football, but not as pointed as a modern-day Rugby ball.

By the 1860s such well-known clubs as Liverpool, Blackheath, Richmond and Sale had been formed. In 1863 Richmond and Blackheath played each other for the first time in what is the longest-surviving regular fixture.

Having spread throughout the British Isles, Rugby was ready to be taken abroad to the colonies. Canada formulated its first set of Rugby rules in 1864 and it was not long afterwards that the game was taken to New Zealand, South Africa and Australia. The Rugby gospel was spread by the public school and university players in the guise of colonial service officials who took with them the message that Rugby was 'a game for ruffians played by gentlemen'. Why countries such as New Zealand and South Africa should take to the game so particularly remains one of sport's great mysteries. And at times, when those two nations have proved invincible, there must have been some regrets at taking the game to their shores in the first place!

As the game grew, it moved away from its 'upper crust' image and was played by the working classes. Nevertheless, there was no desire to adopt any form of professionalism, which was creeping into the Association game.

A need to control the rapidly spreading game saw the inaugural meeting of the Rugby Football Union at the Pall Mall Restaurant, London on 26 January 1871. Twenty clubs attended the inaugural meeting. The sport's first governing body was so well organized and dominant that within ten years of its formation it had instituted what are still regarded as some of the game's top fixtures. The first was the international, a twenty-a-side affair, between Scotland and England, which took place at Raeburn Place, Edinburgh on 27 March 1871. The following year saw the first Oxford versus Cambridge 'Varsity Match'. England played Ireland for the first time in 1875 and that same year the Hospitals' Cup was founded. In 1877 Scotland played Ireland for the first time and by 1883 Wales had joined the international scene, and played each of the other home countries.

Rugby rivalled Association football in popularity with the working man in the North of England, the West Country and Wales. But in Scotland and the London area, Rugby football remained the recreation of the public schoolboy and university student.

Rugby football has always been firm in its defence of its amateur principles. In 1879 it started allowing players expenses of one shilling (5p) for playing in internationals, and later permitted the payment of expenses to players travelling to away matches. But at no time has it allowed payment of compensation for loss of earnings. However, players with certain clubs in the north of England, having lost wages through playing Rugby on Saturday, pressed for payment in lieu of wages but this was not acceptable to the Rugby Football Union. As a result, Northern clubs broke away from the Rugby Union and in 1895 they formed the Northern Rugby Union. And so came about the biggest split in football since 1863 when the Rugby game split from the Association game. We now have amateur Rugby, which was Rugby Union, and professional Rugby, which we now call Rugby League, played alongside Rugby Union in four counties in the north of England.

The amateur code was strong enough to withstand the withdrawal of some of its Northern members and, despite the setback, went on to become one of the great international sports of the twentieth century.

By the time of the split, international Rugby had expanded, and in 1890 the International Rugby Board was set up. It was not until many years later, however, that it became the world governing body for the sport.

A team of New Zealand Maoris visited Britain in 1888 and between March and November that year the first British tourists visited New Zealand and Australia. They were led by Robert Seddon, who sadly lost his life in a boating accident in New South Wales during the tour. Although the tour had the blessing of the Rugby Football Union, it was not under their direct control. It saw the British team lose just two of its 35 matches and was the first of 22 tours made by the British Lions.

Back home, the International Championship, which is still the highlight of the season, was first contested in 1884 by the four home countries. England were the inaugural winners. It became a five nations tournament, as it is today, in 1910 when France became the fifth nation. The French

The fast, long, accurate spin pass of Robert Jones of Wales has marked him as a scrum half of world class ability.

took to the game after British students had taken Rugby across the Channel around 1870.

In 1905 the New Zealand All Blacks were the first fully representative international team to tour Great Britain and they showed a superiority that has diminished very little in all those years. They lost only one of 32 matches and scored 55 points against Devon, the County Champions (the county championship had been introduced in 1889).

When the second All Blacks visited British shores in 1924 they went one better, winning all 28 matches and scoring more than 650 points. Their vast superiority in technique, fitness and all-round teamwork left the British game far behind.

The South Africans were also teaching the 'founders' of the game a thing or two as the British Lions struggled on their 1903, 1910 and 1924 tours. When the South Africans made the opposite journey, to Britain, in 1906-07 and 1912-13 they played a total of 54 matches and lost just 5.

There are eight major Rugby-playing nations, who form the International Board Countries: England, Ireland, Scotland, Wales, France, New Zealand, Australia and South Africa. In addition, countries like Argentina, Canada, Fiji, Italy, Japan, Romania, Tonga, the USA and Western Samoa are ranked as strong 'second division' nations.

Of the top eight, New Zealand, South Africa and Wales have been the game's most outstanding nations over the years. Why? Because Rugby Union is the national game in each of those countries. Elsewhere, Scotland and England have soccer, Ireland has hurling and Gaelic football, Australia has Rugby League and Australian Rules and France has cycling, soccer, motor racing . . . in fact a bit of everything!

At club level there were no criteria for deciding which was the best team until 1971-72, when the Rugby Football Union launched a knockout competition for English club sides, the John Player Cup (known as the Pilkington Cup from 1988-89). Wales introduced their counterpart, the Schweppes Welsh Cup, the same year. In England, teams like Coventry, Gosforth, Leicester and Bath have proved great English champions. And in Wales, Neath, Llanelli, Newport, Swansea, Cardiff and Bridgend have been dominant.

The English County Championship, for so

long regarded as the game's second most important tournament in England after the International Championship, was introduced in 1889. Since then it has been run in various formats. Under the current system, the fifth, counties are graded according to superiority with promotion and relegation each season. The top four teams play-off and the two finalists meet at Twickenham, England's national stadium, towards the end of the season.

Yorkshire were the first champions, and Gloucestershire hold the record for the most wins, fifteen. Between 1958 and 1966 Warwickshire completely dominated the championship, winning it seven times in eight years.

Other popular English competitions are the Services competition, in which the three armed services, Army, Navy and Air Force, play each other on a round-robin basis each season; the Middlesex Sevens, an end-of-season knockout tournament for seven-a-side teams played at Twickenham, often in front of crowds in excess of 50,000, and the Hospitals' Cup for teams representing hospitals up and down the country.

Most Rugby-playing countries have their own championships. In Australia the top prize is the Sydney Premiership, won a record 21 times by University. New Zealand's senior competition is the Ranfurly Shield, an inter-provincial challenge competition, first held in 1904. The state which wins the shield then accepts challenges from other states. The most successful number of defences is twenty-six by Auckland (1960-63) and Canterbury (1982-85). Australia and New Zealand are old rivals on the Rugby field and contest the Bledisloe Cup, named after Lord Bledisloe, former governor-general of New Zealand, who donated the trophy in 1931. New Zealand have dominated the series.

The other stronghold of Rugby is South Africa. The game was first played there in 1862 and the leading competition is the Currie Cup, which is an inter-provincial tournament. It was first held in 1889, and Western Province have won it a record twenty-eight times.

In Scotland, the Club Championship (organized on a league basis) was instituted in 1974 and has proved very popular. The Rugby Football Union resisted the temptation to introduce a similar structure in England. However, in 1985 they approved a plan for two senior divisions, known as Merit Tables (A & B) to allow a promotion and relegation system for leading teams. A third senior clubs division was added in the 1986-87 season and the competition is now open to all clubs in membership. The Courage Clubs Championship, with 1,160 clubs playing in 108 leagues with promotion and relegation at all levels, is believed to be the largest league competition in the world.

Rugby Union made one of its greatest advances in 1987 when the first World Cup was held with victory eventually going to New Zealand. The 1991 World Cup produced sensational rugby finishing with a great final, where Australia defeated England.

That is Rugby at the top level. But, whether it be at that level or at local club level, the principles are the same: to enjoy the game and uphold the amateur spirit.

Club rugby is fun, and that belief should extend beyond the eighty minutes' playing time. Rugby is a great social event and the friendship created off the field (and generally on it) leads to a great after-the-match atmosphere. Most clubs have more than one team and there is plenty of scope for the enthusiastic junior to get into his local team, normally starting in the fifth team (or whatever) and progressing through the ranks.

If you want to join a club, go along and watch your local team one Saturday and approach their secretary with a view to joining the club. You will be made most welcome, provided you intend playing the game in the spirit which it has maintained since the day, back in 1823, when William Webb Ellis picked up the ball at Rugby School and ran with it.

EQUIPMENT & TERMINOLOGY

The pitch

Rugby is played on a rectangular field with a maximum width of 69m (75yd) and a maximum length of 100m (109yd). The dimensions should be as near as possible to these figures but, naturally, local conditions may dictate variations.

The field of play is bounded by touch-lines along each side, and goal-lines at each end. The lines do not form part of the field of play. At each end of the field of play, and extending a maximum of 22m (24yd) from the goal-line, is an in-goal area. The goal-line forms part of the in-goal area but the dead-ball line does not form part of it. The in-goal area, together with the field of play, forms the playing area. The playing enclosure is the playing area, and a reasonable area surrounding it.

The playing area must be grass-covered, or made of clay or sand if grass is not available. Whatever the surface, it must be safe and free from hard objects.

Pitch markings

A halfway line is drawn across the width of the pitch at a point halfway between the goal-lines. Twenty-two metres (24yd) from each goal-line is another line, again the width of the pitch. This is called the 22-metre

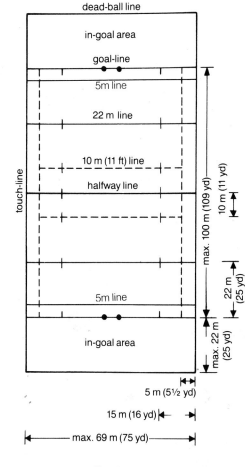

Field of play.

line (the old 25-yard line!) . . . what else would you call it?

A broken line is marked on the pitch 5m (5½yd) from, and parallel to, each of the touch-lines. These extend the length of the pitch. Similar markings are drawn across the pitch parallel to the halfway line and 10m (11yd) to either side of it. These lines are known as the 10-metre lines.

Short lines intersect the halfway line, 10-metre lines and 22-metre lines at a point 15m (16yd) from each touch-line.

Flags

These are positioned at points around the playing area. They are essential at each of the four corners of the field of play, and the recommended height of the flag-sticks is 1.2m (4ft). Flags should also be positioned at each corner of the playing enclosure and at a point outside the touch-line on each side of the field, and adjacent to the 22-metre and halfway lines.

Goalposts

The goals are normally constructed of wood and are in an 'H' formation. The height of the posts varies, and can be any height

above the stipulated minimum of 3.4m (11ft). In practice, most are between 7.5 and 9m (25 and 30ft). The distance between the two uprights is 5.6m (18ft) and the bottom of the posts should be padded to prevent injury. The two posts are joined by a crossbar which is 3m (10ft) above the ground, measured from the ground to the top edge of the crossbar. The crossbar should not extend beyond the posts.

The unbroken lines show the dimensions of the goalposts as per the laws of the game. The broken lines show the height of a typical set of uprights.

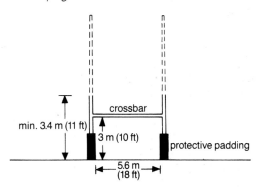

Positions of flags.

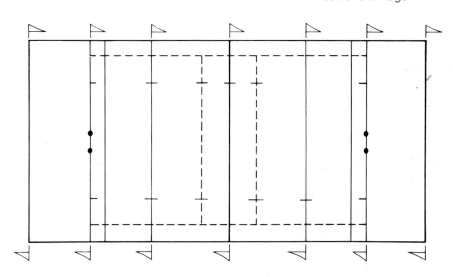

The ball

The Rugby ball is oval, and is made up of four panels stitched together. Originally made of leather, modern-day balls are made out of synthetic materials that are less likely to retain the water in wet conditions. The dimensions of the ball are:

Length: 280–300mm (11–12in)
Circumference: (length-wise): 780–790mm (30–31in)
Circumference: (width-wise): 580–620mm (23–24in)
Weight: 400–440g (14–16oz)

Smaller sizes may be adopted for junior schoolboys.

Player's equipment

Although Rugby football is a tough game, players do not wear protective padding like their American football counterparts. In fact, the wearing of shoulder pads strapped in position is not permitted. Players may wear protection on their shoulders only if the player has suffered an injury and the referee gives permission for the wearing of such pads, but they must only take the form of cotton wool, sponge or similar soft material . . . doesn't that make the gridiron boys look like a bunch of 'softies'? To make the Rugby player look even more 'butch', he doesn't wear the metal protective helmet of the gridiron footballer. He can, however, wear a protective skull-cap if he wishes.

Boots

At one time Rugby boots were large heavy leather items coming well above the ankle to give protection. Boots with ankle protectors are still available, but are much more light-weight. However, the majority of modern players wear the lower-cut boot similar to those worn by soccer players. These are popular with the three-quarters and wingmen, because they can gain extra pace when running.

The laws stipulate the length of studs. Players should wear boots with longer studs in soft ground, and small studs in harder ground. Take great care of your boots, they are not cheap to replace. Clean them after each match, and polish them regularly.

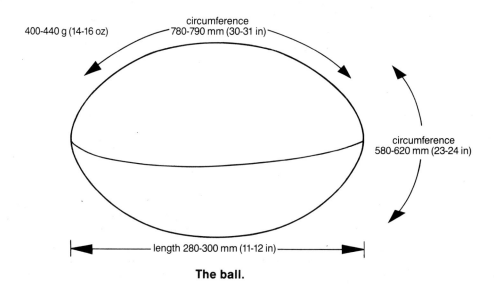

The ball.

Boots.

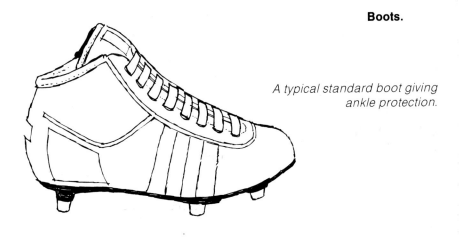

A typical standard boot giving ankle protection.

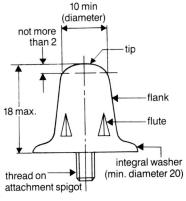

10 min (diameter)

not more than 2

tip

18 max.

flank

flute

thread on attachment spigot

integral washer (min. diameter 20)

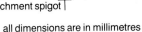
all dimensions are in millimetres

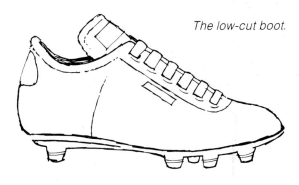

The low-cut boot.

The legal restrictions of the studs.

Shirts, shorts and socks

All players from the same team wear identical clothing; when playing for the fifth team of your local club this may not turn out to be the case. Then a variety of different coloured shorts and socks will be in evidence, but at least the shirts should all be the same colour. Incidentally, if you watch the Barbarians in action you will see that they do not all wear the same-colour socks. Before you start thinking they should be able to afford to kit their team in the same outfits,

there is a reason for this: the Barbarians are a representative side and each player wears his club or national socks.

Players should wear a number on their shirt for identification purposes, and shirts should be numbered 1–15. Two famous clubs, Leicester and Bristol, do not have numbers on their shirts but letters instead. .

That is about the extent of a Rugby player's equipment. The next step is to introduce you to the terminology you will encounter as you watch and play a game.

RUGBY UNION

The strip.

RUGBY UNION · TERMINOLOGY

Advantage law   The discretion of the referee to allow play to continue after an infringement if he thinks that stopping play would penalize the non-offending team even further.

All Blacks   Name given to the touring New Zealand team.

Ankle tap   A method of bringing down a ball-carrier by touching his ankle, thus unbalancing him. You must tap him with your hand – you cannot trip him with your foot.

Attacking team   See *Defending team.*

Backs   Those players who take up a position behind the scrum.

Blind side   The opposite side of the field to where the backs line out from a scrum, line-out, ruck or maul.

Charge down   The blocking of an opponent's kick with the hands, arms or body. If the ball subsequently touches the ground it is *not* penalized as a knock-on.

Conversion   A successful kick over the crossbar following a try. The kick is made from a mark in line with the point where the try was scored. A conversion is worth two points.

Dead   The ball is dead when not in play.

Defending team   The term used to describe the team in whose half of the field play comes to a stop. The opposing team is then known as the *attacking team.*

Dribbling   Controlled kicking of the ball along the ground, soccer-style. It is allowed in Rugby and at one time formed an important part of the game, but not so much these days.

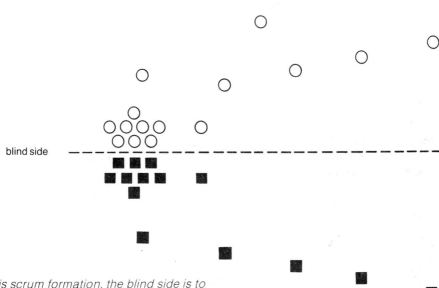

blind side

At this scrum formation, the blind side is to the left of the scrummage.

The drop-kick.

Drop-kick A drop-kick is made by dropping the ball from the hand (or hands) and kicking it at the first rebound after it touches the ground.

Dropped goal A goal scored from a drop-kick while in open play, as opposed to a kick from the ground.

Drop-out A method of re-starting play from either the 22-metre line, or centre-spot, by means of a drop-kick.

Dummy Pretending to pass the ball to another player while keeping possession of it.

Fair catch If a player catches the ball when stationary and with both feet on the ground, on his own side of the 22-metre line, and catches the ball cleanly from a kick, knock-on or throw-forward by an opponent, he can make a *fair catch* by exclaiming 'Mark!'. A free-kick is awarded from such a catch.

Flankers The two forwards who should have the greatest mobility and be able to leave the scrum quickly and get to the loose ball.

Fly-half See *Outside-half.*

Forward A player who packs down in the scrum or forms part of the line-out. The maximum number of forwards permitted is eight in teams in which players are under 19 years.

Forward pass An illegal pass or throw in a forward direction. It is officially called a *throw forward* but generally is referred to as a forward pass.

Free-kick A kick is awarded to a player making a *fair catch*. The person making the catch must take the kick and it must be on or behind the mark made by him. A free-kick is also awarded for certain offences at scrum, ruck and line-out. The kick can take the form of place-kick, punt or drop-kick.

Front row The three forwards who comprise the front row of a scrum.

Full-back The last line of defence, he adopts a position behind the other backs. He is also part of the attack when needed. The full-back is often a team's regular goal-kicker.

Garryowen An *Up-and-under* named after the famous Irish club of the same name.

Goal A goal is the combination of a try and successful conversion. The two are worth six points.

Half-backs The scrum-half and fly-half are the half-backs.

Hand-off A way of fending off a tackler by pushing him away with the open hand.

You can 'hand-off' an opponent to avoid being tackled.

Hooker   The forward in the middle of the front line of the scrum. He is the one who attempts to hook the ball out of the scrum with his foot.

Kick-off   A place-kick from the centre of the half-way line. A kick-off starts each period of play and is also taken by the defending team after a goal has been scored.

Knock-on   When the ball bounces forward off the hand or arm of a player attempting to catch or pick it up, that is a knock-on. If it bounces sideways or back it is not a knock-on.

Line-of-touch   This is an imaginary line in the field of play at right angles to the touch-line through the place where the ball is to be thrown in at a line-out.

Line-out   When the ball goes out of play over the touch-line, play is restarted with a line-out. The two sets of opposing forwards line up at right-angles to the touch-line and parallel to each other. The ball must be thrown straight between the two lines of players.

The line-out

Player A will normally be the opposite number to the thrower. He will take up position as shown to mark the thrower on the blind-side in case he gets the ball palmed from the line-out.

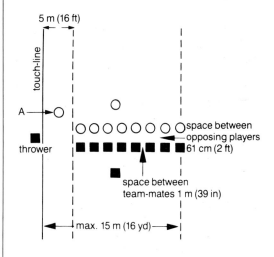

Lions Name given to the touring British Isles team. To be selected for the British Lions is the highest honour in the British game.

Lock forwards The second row of forwards.

Loose-head prop The prop forward who scrums down on the side of the pack nearest to where his scrum-half puts the ball into the scrum.

Mark (i) The mark is the place on the pitch at which a free-kick or penalty kick is awarded. (ii) The call made by a player making a *fair catch*.

Maul A scrimmage of players from both teams made around a player carrying the ball. If he drops the ball to the ground the maul then becomes a *ruck*.

Number eight The forward who scrums down at the back of the scrum. He is so-called because he wears the No. 8

Unlike the drop-kick, the punt is kicked before the ball touches the ground.

jersey . . . not at Leicester or Bristol, that is!

Offside Basically, a player is offside if he is in front of the ball which has been kicked or touched or is being carried by one of the player's team behind him. The rule will be explained fully in the Game Guide section.

Outside-half The back who acts as the link between the scrum-half and the rest of the back players. Also known as a *fly-half*.

Overlap When the team in possession has more players in attack than there are defenders to oppose them.

Pack (i) The term used to describe the forwards. (ii) Going down for a scrum.

Penalty goal A goal scored from a penalty kick. It is worth three points.

Penalty kick Awarded for an infringement of the laws. The non-offending team may have an attempt at goal if they wish. The penalty kick does not have to be a place-kick but can take the form of a punt, drop-kick or tap.

Penalty try The referee can, at his discretion, award a try if a player is fouled or obstructed when a try would probably have resulted. All conversion attempts after a penalty try are taken from a point directly in front of the posts.

Place-kick A place-kick is made by kicking the ball from the ground after it has been specifically placed there for the purpose of making such a kick. It can be held in position by a team-mate if so required.

Prop forwards The two front-row forwards on either side of the hooker.

Punt A punt is made by dropping the ball from the hand (or hands) and kicking it before it touches the ground.

'Round-the-corner' kick

When taking a dead-ball kick, the kicker can either adopt a straight run-up, as in A, or a 'round-the-corner' run-up as in B.

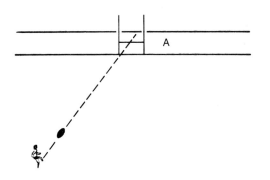

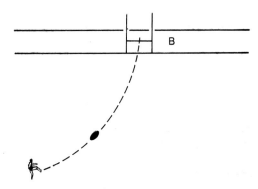

Replacement A substitute player allowed onto the field in place of an injured player.

Round-the-corner kick A style of goal-kicking whereby the kicker approaches the ball in a curving run-up (more like in soccer) as opposed to approaching the ball in a straight line.

Ruck A scrimmage formed by the opposing sets of forwards around the ball after it has been grounded.

Scrum (also known as scrummage and scrimmage) A means of re-starting play, usually following an infringement. At least five players must form the scrum, but usually all eight forwards interlock in a 3-4-1 formation. The two sets of front-row forwards interlock with each other.

Scrum-half The link between a team's forwards and the backs. He is responsible for monitoring the scrum and getting possession as soon as he can, and then quickly deciding what type of play to build up: either a passing one, or a kicking one.

Second row The two forwards who form the second row of the scrum.

Set-pieces The *scrum* and *line-out* are set-pieces.

Sevens A form of Rugby played on a full-sized pitch but with only seven players per side. Often very fast, it calls for maximum fitness from the competing players.

Springboks The name of the touring South African international team.

Stand-off half Another name for the *fly-half.*

Tackle The stopping of an opponent who is running with the ball.

Tap kick A kick of only a few inches made after a re-start by a player to himself; he then either runs with the ball, or passes or kicks it.

Three-quarters The name given to the two centres and two wingers, i.e. the four backs between the outside-half and the full-back.

Throw forward   The official name for a *forward pass*.

Tight-head prop   The opposite to *loose-head prop*. He is the prop forward on the side of the scrum opposite to where the opposing scrum-half puts the ball into the scrum.

Touch-down   If a defending player grounds the ball in his own in-goal area it is a touch-down. It is *not* a try, and does not score any points. The term is often incorrectly used to describe a try.

Touch-in-goal   When the ball goes out of play behind the goal-line.

Touch-line   The two lines down each side of the pitch are the touch-lines. Any ball that touches the lines or the ground beyond is out of play and said to be *in touch*.

Triple Crown   If one of the four home countries defeats the other three in a season's international championship they achieve the Triple Crown. It is only a mythical trophy.

Try   When a player grounds the ball in the opposing in-goal area he is said to have scored a try. It is worth four points. All tries are followed by goal attempts (conversions) and if successful the try is re-named a goal.

Up-and-under   A high kick that is used to put pressure on the opposing team. While the ball is in the air the kicker's team-mates, generally the backs, advance upfield ready to meet the landing ball.

Wing forward   See *Flankers*.

Wing three-quarters   The two outside backs. They are usually the fastest players in a team.

With your new-found knowledge of Rugby terms we can now take you into the Game Guide, a look at the rules and how the game is played. If you have any problems with the terminology, just keep referring back to this chapter.

One of the few French players to break through to world recognition in the early 1990s is Olivier Roumat, a tall, strong and hard-running forward whose presence at the line out and in loose play greatly assists his team.

THE GAME – A GUIDE

The object of a game of Rugby Union is to score more points than the opposing team as a result of carrying, passing or kicking the ball. The team scoring the most points wins a match. Should the scores be level then the result is a draw. Rarely is extra-time played in Rugby Union.

No matter what the outcome of the match you should always remember that Rugby is a gamed played by gentlemen, and the law and spirit of the game should be maintained at all times.

The match officials

A game is controlled by a referee and two touch-judges.

The **referee** is responsible for making sure the laws of the game are fairly applied. He also keeps a note of the time and the score. He is the sole arbitrator and his decisions are final. He also has the power to allow the advantage rule if, after an infringement, the non-offending team would lose their advantage by his stopping play.

We cannot stress enough how important it is to accept the referee's decision as final. It is pointless arguing, you will only get into more trouble.

There are times when referees make mistakes (sadly nobody has made a computer capable of controlling a Rugby match yet) but there is nothing you can do about it. Just try refereeing some time . . . you will then appreciate how difficult the job is. Just imagine trying to be fully conversant with all the rules of the game *and* having to decide when to apply them.

To make the referee's job that bit easier he is assisted by two **touch-judges**, one for each touch-line. They remain 'in touch' until a goal attempt when they both take up a position behind the goal to rule whether a kick is successful or not.

Using his flag to attract the referee's attention, the touch-judge advises when the ball and/or a player goes into touch. He indicates where the ball or player crossed the touch-line and indicates which team has the throw-in. In certain senior games he reports to the referee incidents of foul play.

Team positions

A team consists of fifteen players. Replacements (substitutes) are allowed in place of injured players. The fifteen players are divided into two groups, forwards and backs.

Forwards Their role is to gain possession of the ball and get it to their backs who should try and develop a running play. There are eight forwards in a team: a hooker, two

REFEREE'S SIGNALS

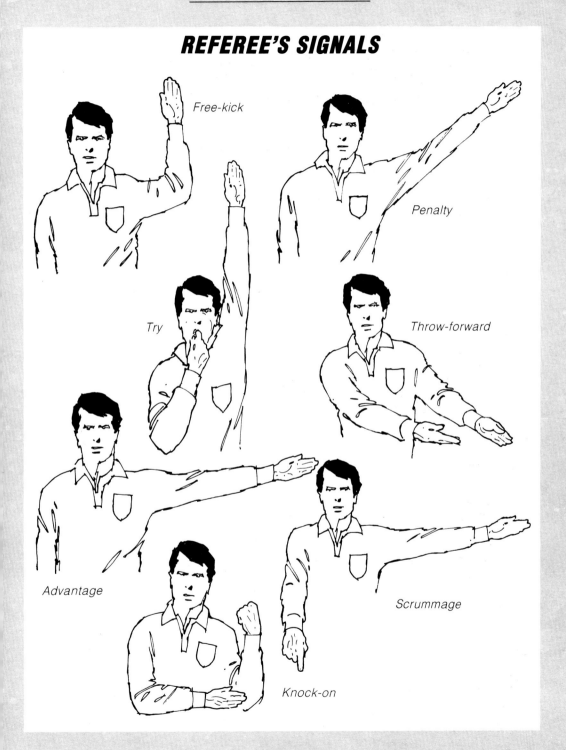

Free-kick

Penalty

Try

Throw-forward

Advantage

Scrummage

Knock-on

Touch-judge's signals

Goal

Found touch

Foul play

props, two locks, two flanks and a No. 8. The forwards are regarded as the 'heavyweight' brigade of any team, and tend to tip the scales at a few pounds more than the backs!

When a scrummage is formed (see page 34) all eight players can be used (less than eight can form a scrum, but it is more practicable to utilize all eight). Most teams adopt a standard 3-4-1 formation at the scrummage, with the hooker being the central character.

The laws governing the scrum will be explained in detail later.

The team positions

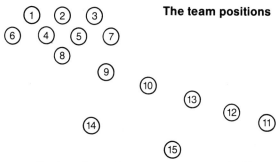

Front-row forwards
1 – 3 Props
2   Hooker

Second-row forwards
4 and 5 Lock forwards
6 and 7 Flankers

Back-row forward(s)
8 No. 8 forward

Half-backs
9 Scrum-half
10 Outside-half

Three-quarters
11 Right wing three-quarter
12 Right centre three-quarter
13 Left centre three-quarter
14 Left wing three-quarter

Full-back
15 Full-back

Backs   These are the more mobile members of the team. They are the ones who have the pace to create running moves in an effort to score points.

Perhaps the most important of the backs is the scrum-half. His job is to act as the link between the forwards and other backs. He must be quick-thinking and be able to spot an opening to get one or all of his fellow backs into an attacking play.

The backs play two roles: those of attacker and defender. They should be good tacklers as well as good handlers, passers and runners.

Starting a match

Play starts with the toss of a coin between the two captains. The winning captain can either choose to kick-off, or pick which end of play to defend in the first half.

Play lasts eighty minutes, divided into two equal halves of forty minutes (in junior matches this can be reduced upon agreement by both sides). At half-time, an interval of up to five minutes is allowed, and when play resumes the teams change halves. When 'no-side' is called by the referee it signals the end of a match.

The seven-a-side game is another popular form of Rugby. Known as 'Sevens', it is played on a full-size pitch and lasts seven minutes each way, with a one-minute break at half-time. Major finals (e.g. in the Middlesex Sevens) last ten minutes each way.

In all matches, play starts with a kick-off, which is a place-kick taken from the centre of the halfway line by the team having the right to the kick-off. At the start of play in the second half the other team kicks off.

If, from the kick-off, the ball goes directly into touch, lands directly in the in-goal area, or directly over (or on) the dead-ball line then the opposing team has the choice of either (i) accepting the kick, (ii) asking for it to be re-taken, or (iii) asking for a scrummage at the centre-spot.

At the kick-off, the kicker's team must be behind the ball at the time of the kick. If not, the referee can order a scrummage at the centre. The opposing team must stand on or behind their 10-metre line.

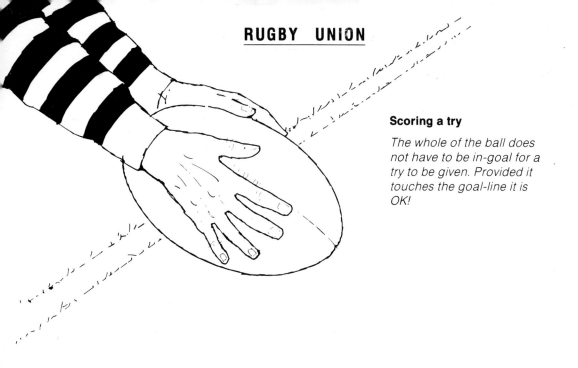

Scoring a try

The whole of the ball does not have to be in-goal for a try to be given. Provided it touches the goal-line it is OK!

Scoring points

There are four ways of scoring points:

1 Try .... worth 5 points
2 Goal after a try .... worth 2 points
3 Penalty kick .... worth 3 points
4 Dropped goal .... worth 3 points

Try   A try is scored by grounding the ball in the opposing in-goal area. For the ball to be grounded, the player must be holding it in his hand(s) or arm(s) when he brings it into contact with the ground.

The ball can also be deemed to be grounded if a player falls on the ball, but the front of the body from waist to neck must make contact with the ball for a successful grounding.

The referee has the right to award a **penalty try** if he feels that, by an infringement of the laws, a player was prevented from scoring a try. It is still worth four points and, for the purpose of the subsequent goal attempt, is deemed to have been scored between the posts. The referee can also award the kick from between the posts if, after the ball was grounded for a legitimate try, he felt further advantage could have been gained had there not been an infringement at the time of the grounding.

Goal attempt after a try   Every try is further rewarded with a kick at goal, which can increase the score by another two points. The kick is taken from a point on the playing area level with the point where the ball was grounded.

The kick can be either a place-kick or drop-kick, and all players on the kicker's team must be behind the ball at the time of the kick. Another player from his side (a placer) can be positioned to hold the ball in place (usually when there is a strong wind); he is exempt from the behind-the-ball rule.

At the kick, the defending team must stand behind their own goal-line. Once the kicker commences his run-up, or starts to make the kick, the defenders can advance forward and jump in an attempt to prevent the goal being scored.

Free kick   A free kick is a kick awarded for a fair-catch or to the non-offending team as stated in the Laws. A goal may not be scored from a free kick.

The conversion attempt

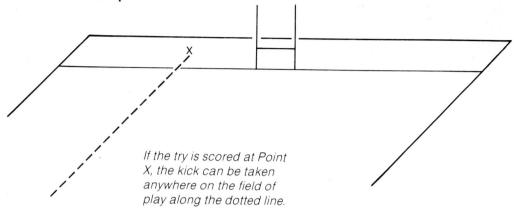

If the try is scored at Point X, the kick can be taken anywhere on the field of play along the dotted line.

The team awarded a free kick may not score a dropped goal until after the ball next becomes dead or the ball has been played or touched by an opposing player.

For an infringement it may be taken by any player of the non-offending team.

It may be taken by any form of kick provided that the kicker, if holding the ball, must propel it out of his hands or, if the ball is on the ground, he must propel it a visible distance from the mark. He may keep his hand on the ball while kicking it.

Penalty kick   A penalty kick is a kick (not necessarily at goal) by the non-offending team following an infringement of the rules.

The rules for a penalty apply in the same way as they do for the goal attempt after the try. The kick must be taken, however, at or behind the point where the infringement took place.

If the kicking team commits any breach during the penalty then the referee shall order a scrummage at the mark where the kick was awarded. If the non-kicking team commits any breach then the penalty is taken from a point 10m (11yd) in front of the mark, or 5m (16ft) from the goal-line, whichever is nearer. However, if the kick is successful during or after the infringement by a member of the non-kicking team, then the score shall count.

The non-offending team does not have to take a kick, and can elect to have a scrummage instead; if so, they have the right to put the ball in.

Dropped goal   A player can, at any time during open play, have an attempt at kicking a goal by means of a drop-kick. The successful kick is worth three points. The kick must be a drop-kick, and not a punt. All restarts must be by a Drop Goal. Possession is crucial in Rugby, just as it is in many other team sports. You will have gathered already that scoring a try can be worth six points, with the successful goal-kick after the try. So, the principal aim is to work the ball upfield by a series of passing moves, or kicks, and get away from defending players in order to reach the opposing in-goal area to ground the ball and score a try. However, games are won without a team scoring a try – goal-kicking alone can win matches. Remember, it is points that wins matches, not who scores the most tries. most tries.

There is no finer sight than a line of backs supporting each other as they weave their way through the opposing team and fluently pass the ball, one to another, before scoring an impressive try. But such moves are ones to be savoured on rare occasions. In practice, advancement up the field is by a series of kicks or short passes followed by a series of tackles, which result in possession being retained, or regained, by way of rucks and mauls.

Play is kept as fluent as possible, but it occasionally stops for one reason or another. Let's have a look at some of those reasons why play has to be halted.

HALTS · IN · PLAY
WHEN · & · WHY

Throw forward

The ball *must always* be passed sideways or backwards in Rugby. It cannot be passed forward. If it is, then it is known as a throw forward, and the player committing the offence will be penalized. If the throw forward is intentional then a penalty is awarded from the point where the infringement took place. If it was unintentional then a scrummage shall be formed at the place of the infringement.

Knock-on

The ball must always be gathered cleanly. If a player loses possession of the ball, and it travels forward towards the opposing goal-line, or it strikes a player's hand and travels forward, then it is a knock-on and is penalized in the same way as the throw forward unless the player recovers the ball before it has touched the ground or another player.

These incidents arise out of passing moves. But what happens if the ball-carrier is tackled?

The tackle

First of all, you must attempt to play the ball, in other words try and pass to a team-mate. If you cannot make a pass then you must release the ball immediately and get up, or move away; you cannot touch the ball again, or interfere in play until you are back on your feet. If you do, you will be penalized and a penalty kick awarded to the opposing team.

After the ball is released a **ruck**, or **maul**, often forms around the ball. This is like an impromptu scrum with at least one player from either side closing around the ball, which is somewhere between them. When the ball becomes unplayable or becomes stationary a scrummage shall be ordered and the ball inserted by the team who were not initially in possession.

A knock-on

If the ball goes forward after striking the player's hand(s) it is a 'knock-on' . . .

. . . however, if after hitting his hands the ball bounces vertically or behind the vertical it is not a knock-on. If it should then bounce forward it is still not a knock-on.

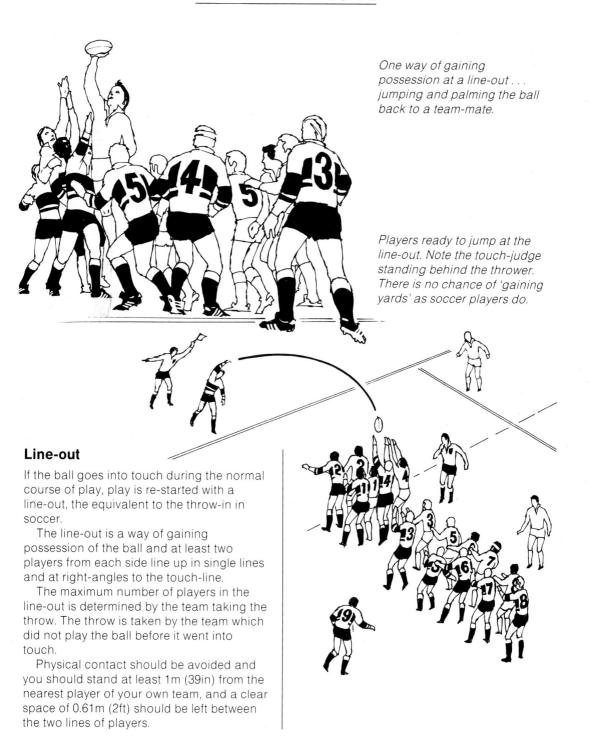

One way of gaining possession at a line-out . . . jumping and palming the ball back to a team-mate.

Players ready to jump at the line-out. Note the touch-judge standing behind the thrower. There is no chance of 'gaining yards' as soccer players do.

Line-out

If the ball goes into touch during the normal course of play, play is re-started with a line-out, the equivalent to the throw-in in soccer.

The line-out is a way of gaining possession of the ball and at least two players from each side line up in single lines and at right-angles to the touch-line.

The maximum number of players in the line-out is determined by the team taking the throw. The throw is taken by the team which did not play the ball before it went into touch.

Physical contact should be avoided and you should stand at least 1m (39in) from the nearest player of your own team, and a clear space of 0.61m (2ft) should be left between the two lines of players.

The line-out starts from a point 5m (16ft) from the touch-line where the throw is being taken, and stretches to a point 15m (16yd) away. Any player beyond 15m (16yd) is not deemed to be in the line-out.

The ball must be thrown straight between the two lines of players; you cannot try to gain an advantage by throwing towards the side of the line-out containing your own players. Once the ball has been thrown, the two sets of forwards jump and try to get possession of the ball. Possession can be obtained by:

1 Jumping for the ball and using both hands or the inside of the arm to catch or deflect the ball
2 Getting possession from a ruck or maul which may occur after the throw-in

The point from where the throw is taken varies under different conditions. It is taken from the point where the ball went out of play if:

1 It goes into touch from a penalty kick.
2 It goes into touch from a free-kick.
3 It is from a kick made within 22m (24yd) of the kicker's goal-line.

If it should go into touch following a kick and it does not meet those conditions then the throw is taken from a point level with the place where the ball was kicked. However, if it crosses (or touches) the touch-line nearer to the kicker's goal (that is, if the ball should travel backwards), then *that* point shall determine from where the throw is taken.

If the ball goes into touch under any other circumstances, then the point where it touches or crosses the touch-line is the point from where the throw is taken.

Any infringement to the line-out rule can result in the opposing team taking the throw or by a scrummage forming. If a scrummage results then it is formed 15m (16yd) from the touch-line along the line-of-touch.

Fair catch (Mark)

A player can make a mark by catching the ball from a kick, knock-on, or throw forward by one of his opponents. He must, however, be stationary, and with both feet on the ground, and on his side of the 22-metre line.

After making a mark, the player has the option of a free-kick which can be either a place, drop or tap-kick. A goal cannot be scored direct from a free-kick. If he chooses

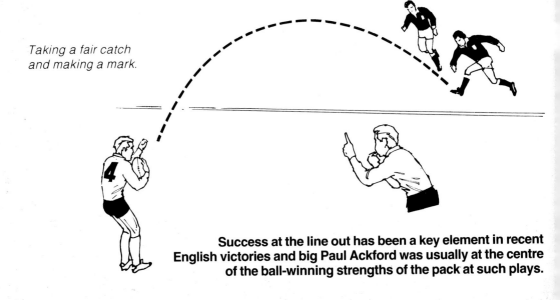

Taking a fair catch and making a mark.

Success at the line out has been a key element in recent English victories and big Paul Ackford was usually at the centre of the ball-winning strengths of the pack at such plays.

The two popular set-scrum formations are:

3-4-1 formation

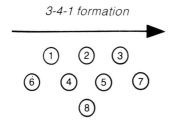

3-3-2 formation

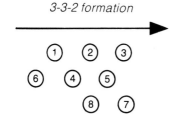

Front-row forwards must bind under the armpits and stay bound until the ball is out of the scrum.

not to take a kick, then his side can elect to have a scrummage instead.

If a player is injured in the process of making a mark and cannot, within one minute, take the kick, a scrummage results with his own side putting the ball in.

Players of the kicking team must be behind the ball at the time of the kick and the opposing team must be on or behind a line parallel to their own goal-line and 10m (11yd) from the mark. Once the kicker places the ball on the ground or starts his run-up or kick, the opposing players can charge.

For any infringement by the kicking team at a mark a scrummage is formed with the opposing team putting the ball in. If an offence is committed by the non-kicking team, then a free kick shall be awarded to the kicking team from a point 10m (11yd) in front of the mark.

Drop-out

The drop-out is a drop-kick taken by the defending team. The kick is taken from anywhere on or behind their own 22m (24yd) line. If taken from behind the 22m line the ball must reach that line from the drop-out. If it does not, the opposing team can ask for it to be re-taken or for a scrummage, formed at the centre of the 22m line.

The drop-out is used to re-start play after a touch-down, (when you ground the ball in your own in-goal area), after the ball has gone into touch-in-goal, or gone over the dead-ball line.

The drop kick is also used for all restarts other than a place kick at the start of each half.

Scrummage

Affectionately known as 'the scrum'. It forms an important part of Rugby Union and the strength of a set of forwards often dictates the advantage one team may gain at scrums. The object at the scrum is to gain possession of the ball and get it out to your own scrum-half so he can engineer an attacking move.

The scrum . . .
a bird's-eye view.

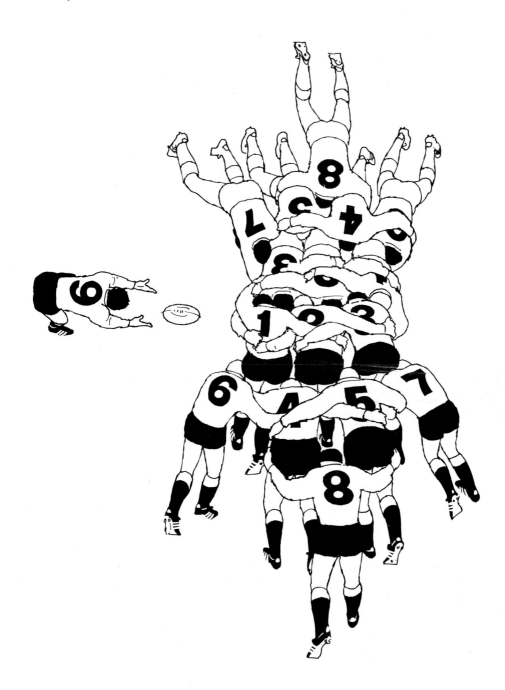

RUGBY UNION

The scrum . . . in action.

The scrum is a heads-down 'free-for-all' between the opposing sets of forwards, who interlock with each other.

Once the scrum is formed, the ball is thrown in by one of the scrum-halves and the hooker (the player in the middle of the front row) attempts to hook the ball back to his team-mates who will, in turn, gradually hook it out to the scrum-half who will have taken up a position at the back, or side, of the scrum.

The most effective way of gaining advantage is by pushing the opposing forwards backwards (a tug-of-war in reverse); this is where a heavy pack comes in useful.

When formed, the scrummage shall take place at the point where any infringement took place (or as near to it as possible). The line of scrummage – the imaginary line between the two sets of front-row forwards, should always be parallel to the goal-lines.

The forwards of each team must not interlock with each other until the scrum-half, or person acting as scrum-half, has the

ball in his possession and is ready to feed the scrum.

The scrum is used to re-start play after certain infringements and can only be formed on the field of play. A scrum cannot be formed in the in-goal area or within 5m (16ft) of the touch-line.

If any infringement by the defending team takes place in their own in-goal area, and the penalty would be a scrum, then the scrummage must be formed 5m (16ft) from the goal-line on the field of play.

A minimum of five players are required from each team to form a scrum. Of that minimum, three players MUST form the front row.

The player putting the ball into the scrum must make sure the ball bounces along the line of scrummage beyond the feet of the nearest player. The ball *must* be put into the scrum in a straight line.

If you think about it logically, there are three players on each front row and it is impossible for them to interlock by putting their heads together . . . their heads must be either to the right or left of the opposing player. This brings us to the question of which players have the right to stand nearest the player putting the ball in. The answer is simple . . . the team who have possession of the ball.

The scrum . . . a worm's-eye view along the tunnel.

How the opposing props may bind.

The laws of the game regarding the scrummage leave it wide open for numerous scrum infringements. If you are putting the ball in, make sure you stand 1m (39in) away from the scrum at the time and put it in straight and fairly, and despatch the ball in one quick movement.

If you are a forward in the scrum you would be advised to digest the following . . . they are just some of the more important scrum infringements:

1 Don't allow your shoulders to fall below the level of your hips if you are a front-rower.
2 Keep both feet on the ground, and you must not cross them until the ball has gone into the 'tunnel' between the two sets of front-row players.
3 Don't raise your foot (if you are a front-rower) until the ball has hit the ground in the tunnel.
4 Don't deliberately kick the ball out of either end of the tunnel.
5 If you are a second- or back-row player do not play the ball while it is in the tunnel.
6 Don't handle the ball in the scrum except for a push-over try or touch-down.
7 Don't deliberately cause the scrum to collapse.
8 Don't deliberately fall, or kneel in the scrum.
9 Don't attempt to gain possession of the ball with any part of your body other than your foot or lower leg.

For breaking any of the scrum laws, you will be penalized with a penalty kick or free kick against you.

Offside

Now for the offside rule. Let's start by making it as simple as possible. In basic terms a player is offside in general play if he is in front of the ball when it is last played by a member of his team.

If play is at a scrummage, ruck, maul or line-out a player is offside if he advances in front of the line for the particular play.

Now let's start getting a bit more technical. Firstly, let's look at the offside rule in general play.

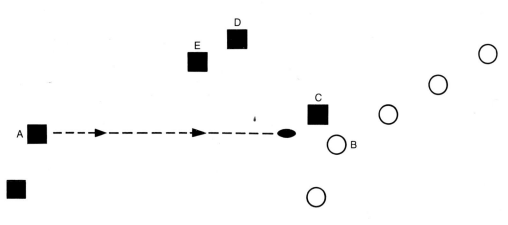

Offside in general play

Player A kicks the ball. As opponent B attempts to catch it, players C, D and E are all in offside positions. E and D are more than 10m (11yd) from B and would not be penalized. C is within 10m (11yd) and the referee would award a penalty.

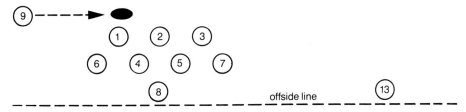

Offside at a scrummage

Player 13 (centre three-quarter) is offside because he is not involved in the scrum and is on the wrong side of the imaginary offside line.

Offside in general play   A player is in an offside *position* if he is in front of the ball when it is kicked, touched, or carried by one of his team-mates. However, there is no penalty for being in an offside *position* unless that player plays the ball, obstructs an opponent or approaches (or remains) within 10m (11yd) of an opponent waiting to play the ball or where the ball pitches.

Any player caught offside is penalized with a penalty kick against him from the spot where he is in the offside position. The non-offending team can, however, elect to have a scrummage instead, taken from the point where the ball was last played.

Offside at a scrummage   A player is offside at the scrum if he joins the scrummage from his opponents' side. A player will also be ruled offside if, not being a player in the scrummage, nor the player throwing in the ball, he does not retire behind the offside line.

The offside line at the scrum (or ruck or maul) is, for each team, an imaginary line drawn parallel with the goal-lines and along a line level with the back foot of the furthermost player on each side of the scrummage.

The player putting the ball into the scrum and his immediate opponent is offside if he remains or places one foot in front of the ball while it is in the scrummage. His

immediate opponent is also offside if he takes up a position on the opposite side of the scrummage in front of the offside line.

Offside at a scrum is penalized with a penalty kick from the place of the infringement.

Offside at a ruck or maul   A player is offside if he joins the ruck or maul from his opponents' side, joins it in front of the ball, or fails to retire behind the offside line *without delay* after deciding not to join the ruck or maul. He is also offside if he leaves the ruck or maul and does not *immediately* retire behind the offside line. He can break from the ruck or maul and return to it, but must do so immediately and rejoin it behind the ball. Any player who advances beyond the offside line without joining the ruck or maul is also offside.

Any infringement and it's a penalty kick from the place of infringement.

If the ruck or maul is at a line-out the above rules apply. A player in the line-out does *not* have to join the ruck or maul. If he doesn't he must get behind the offside line as soon as possible and remain there until the line-out ends.

Offside at a line-out   This is a bit different to the other cases of offside infringements. Firstly, the imaginary offside line for players not in the line-out is now positioned 10m

RUGBY UNION

(11yd) behind the line-of-touch (if the goal-line is within 10m (11yd), then *it* shall be the offside line).

For the purpose of this rule, the only players deemed to be part of the line-out are those in the line, the player taking the throw (and his opposite number) and one other player from each team who stands in a position to catch a ball passed on or knocked back from the line-out. All other players are *not* part of the line-out.

A player not involved in the line-out is offside if he advances with one or both feet beyond the offside line. A player who *is* involved in the line-out is offside if he advances over the line-of-touch before the ball has touched a player or the ground, unless that advancement is done while jumping for the ball. After the ball has touched a player or the ground, the player is offside if he advances in front of the ball unless tackling or attempting to tackle an opponent who took part in the line-out. Remember, we said earlier that the line-out extends to 15m (16yd) from the touch-line. Well, any player involved in the line-out who moves beyond that limit before the end of the line-out shall be offside.

Offside infringements by players in the line-out are penalized with a penalty kick taken 15m (16yd) from the touch-line along the line-of-touch. Offside infringements by players not in the line-out are penalized with a penalty kick taken at least 15m (16yd) from the touch-line and 10m (11yd) behind the line-of-touch.

The person throwing the ball in at the line-out can also be offside and will be penalized if he does not either (a) remain within 5m (16ft) of the touch-line, (b) retire to behind the offside line, (c) join the line-out after the ball has been thrown 5m (16ft), or (d) move into position to receive the ball when passed or knocked back from the line-out, provided no other player from his team is in such a position.

Foul play

The Laws of the Game put foul play under three headings: obstruction, unfair play/repeated infringements, and misconduct/dangerous play.

Commonsense will tell the good player what is unfair and what is foul play.

You cannot charge or push an opponent, other than shoulder-to-shoulder; otherwise it constitutes obstruction.

You cannot wilfully waste time, or wilfully throw the ball from the playing area into touch, touch-in-goal or over the dead-ball line, or regularly infringe the laws. Such acts constitute unfair play.

You cannot strike an opponent or wilfully hack or kick another player. You are not allowed deliberately to cause a scrummage, ruck or maul to collapse. These offences constitute the breaking of the misconduct and dangerous-play rules. Such infringements would receive a caution from the referee. Persistence will result in you being sent off the field of play.

These are just some of the many rules which constitute 'foul play'. If you play the game fairly you need not know, and need never find out, what the other rules are . . .

Remember what we said at the beginning: Rugby was once described as 'a game for ruffians played by gentlemen'. Rugby prides itself in its continuing spirit of hard but fair play. Make sure you play the game with that spirit.

Michael Jones has quickly become a highly regarded flank forward because of his electric pace at scrums and line outs. It is his support play around the field which ranks him amongst the greats, and here he outpaces some of England's fastest to score a try.

RULES CLINIC

How many replacements are allowed during a game?

The most permitted per team is two. In matches between teams of schoolboys, or teams where all players are under 21 years of age, then six per side are permitted. Once a player has been replaced he cannot return to the action.

Rugby is a fast game at times and with 30 players on the field it is inevitable that collisions will occur. But what happens if a player, or indeed the ball, hits the referee?

If the ball, or player carrying the ball, touches the referee then play shall continue unless the referee feels an unfair advantage will be gained by carrying on, in which case

a scrummage will be ordered. If a ball-carrier runs into the referee in his own in-goal area then a touch-down will be awarded. If this happens in the opposing in-goal area then a try will be awarded from the point where the player touched the referee.

You said that from the kick-off the ball must cross the opposing 10-metre line. What happens if it crosses it and a strong wind blows it back?

Play continues as normal.

If a successful kick goes over the crossbar and is then blown back by a strong wind, does the goal still count?

Yes.

Can a goal be scored by rebounding off a post or the crossbar?

Yes.

Can a try be scored from a scrummage close to the goal-line which pushes over the line?

Yes. A try can be scored from a 'push-over' scrummage or ruck, but the ball must be grounded on or over the line.

If a player is tackled and his momentum carries him over the goal-line and he grounds the ball in-goal, is it a try?

Yes.

If you are tackled but your momentum carries you over the goal-line and you ground the ball properly, then a try is awarded.

I understand when scoring a try, in order to make the subsequent kick easier, it is best to ground the ball as near the goalposts as possible. If you ground it, say, near one of the corner-flags and then realise you could have scored nearer the goalposts, can you pick the ball up and reground it?

No. The first place it is grounded must stand.

Is it possible to score an 'own try', like an 'own goal' in soccer?

No. You can ground the ball in your own in-goal area but it is not a try to the opposing team. This is called a touch-down. If you carry the ball into your own in-goal area and then ground the ball play is re-started with a scrummage to the opposing side on the 5-metre line. However, if you are already in your in-goal area, and receive the ball which an opponent has kicked into that area and ground it, play re-starts with a drop-out to your side from the 22-metre line.

. . . Does this, therefore, mean I must ground the ball once I have possession of it in my own in-goal area?

No, you can keep the play flowing and start an attacking move.

Often several players from either side may attempt to ground a loose ball in the in-goal area. What should the referee do if he has a doubt who got to the ball first?

Award a scrummage 5 m (16 ft) from the goal-line. The attacking side puts the ball into the scrummage.

If a ball goes into touch directly from a drop-out, what happens?

The non-kicking team may accept the kick, have the ball dropped-out again or have a scrum formed at the centre of the kicking team's 22-metre line.

If a player charges down a kick is he deemed to have knocked-on?

No, provided he is not trying to catch the ball.

A player can charge down an opponent's kick. If the ball rebounds forward it is not a knock-on.

If a player makes a 'mark' in-goal and elects to have a scrummage, where is it formed – because you said a scrum cannot be formed in-goal?

Well spotted! It is formed at a point 5m (16ft) from the goal-line, and at a point level with the 'mark'.

Is it a knock-on if a player fumbles the ball several times before eventually getting hold of it cleanly?

No, provided he recovers the ball before it touches the ground or another player.

John Eales charges through Irish cover in a typically robust run. Achieving international honours in a great team whilst still very young has shown the regard coaches have for this speedy giant.

In the maul

If only two players 'surround' this ball-carrier they must be from opposite sides.

Once in the maul, the ball-carrier cannot be tackled around the legs. This constitutes dangerous play (causing the maul to collapse).

Once the ball hits the ground the maul becomes a ruck.

What is the difference between a ruck and a maul?

A maul is when one or more players from each team, while on their feet and in physical contact, close around a player carrying the ball. Once the ball-carrier drops the ball to the ground the maul ends and it inevitably becomes a ruck. The ruck is, in effect, an impromptu scrummage.

If a player is in touch can he still get involved in play?

Yes. He may kick or propel the ball with his hand, provided the ball is still in play. If he catches the ball while in touch, however, the ball is deemed to be out of play.

You said that if the ball at a line-out is not thrown in properly then the opposing team takes the throw. But what happens if they don't throw it in properly?

A scrummage shall be formed and the ball put in by the team who had the first throw at the line-out . . . let's hope they can put it into the scrum straight!

What is 'peeling off'?

It happens at a line-out when one or more players move from their position in the line-out to take up a position to catch the ball when passed or knocked-back by a team-mate in the line-out.

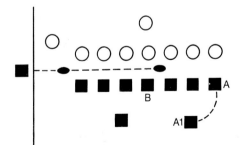

Peeling off

After the throw at the line-out, player A may leave the line and peel-off to position A1 ready to take the palm-back from either B or C.

If a player is, say, on the ground injured and in an offside position and cannot avoid being hit by the ball or ball-carrier, is he still penalized for being offside?

No. It is an 'accidental offside' and consequently the player is not penalized and play shall continue unless that player's team gains an unfair advantage, in which case a scrummage is formed.

Can a player not involved in a line-out take up a position at the end of the line to take a long throw?

Yes, and no. He can, but not until the ball has left the hand of the player throwing the ball. If he moves before then the referee will penalize him for being offside.

When is a player in an offside position brought on-side?

1 When the offside player retreats behind the player of his team who last kicked, touched or carried the ball.
2 When a team-mate carrying the ball runs ahead of him.
3 When a team-mate runs ahead of the offside player after coming from a position where the ball was (or behind it) when it was last kicked.

A player can be played on-side by the opposing team if:

1 An opponent kicks or passes the ball.
2 An opponent carrying the ball has run 5m (16ft).
3 An opponent intentionally touches the ball and does not catch or gather it.

However, a player who is within 10m (11yd) of an opponent waiting to play the ball or where the ball pitches, cannot be played onside by the opposing team. He must retire towards his own goal line until put on side.

Does a kicker have to attempt a shot at goal from a penalty?

No, He may kick the ball in any direction. He can even play the ball again, i.e. tap the ball to himself. However, he must indicate to the referee if he is kicking at goal. Once he has done that he cannot change his mind.

Can a player deliberately throw a ball into touch, touch-in-goal or over the dead-ball line?

No, if he does, a penalty will be awarded. Persistently breaking the law will result in a sending-off.

Can a goal be scored direct from a kick-off?

No, nor can one be scored direct from a drop-out, free-kick or punt.

If a legal pass does not reach its intended player but hits the ground and then bounces forward, is it deemed to be a forward pass?

No, and play continues.

If the ball hits a player's hand or arm and drops vertically to the ground, is it a knock-on?

No, the ball must bounce forward. If it hits any other part of his body, e.g. chest or legs, and then bounces forward then it is not a knock-on, it is a rebound.

Ball out of scrummage

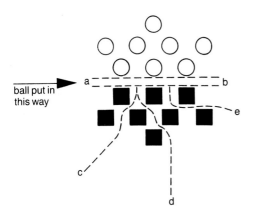

ball put in
this way

*From the scrum the ball cannot come out
between the opposing front-row forwards at
either end of the tunnel (a or b). It can
however follow the courses shown at c, d
and e, and their opposites.*

Where must the ball come out of the scrummage?

Anywhere except either end of the tunnel. If it
comes out at either end the referee will order
it to be re-taken or, if it is deliberately kicked
out he can award a free kick.

Does a penalty kick have to be taken from the point where the infringement took place?

No, it can be taken from behind it. If it is,
then the opposing players must stand 10m
(11yd) behind the point where the infringement occurred, and not 10m (11yd) behind
the place where the kick is taken.

If a kick at goal following a try does not reach the goalposts and stays on the field of play, does play continue in the normal way?

No. It is treated as an unsuccessful attempt
and play re-starts with a drop-out from the
halfway line.

In order to score a try does a player have to take the ball into the in-goal area or can he ground a ball that was already there from, say, a kick?

Yes. He may ground a ball already in the
in-goal area, he does not have to carry it
there.

Placing a penalty kick

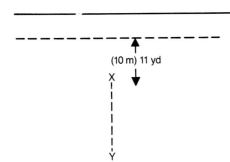

(10 m) 11 yd

*If the offence took place at Point
X, the kick can be taken
anywhere along the line X-Y. The
defenders, however, must stand
behind the line 10m (11yd) from X.*

TECHNIQUE

Rugby is a team game played by fifteen individuals. Before we look at some techniques it would be a good idea to look more closely at each of the individual players on the field and the role each has to play.

The forwards

Hooker   He supports his two props and is the man who attempts to win the ball at the scrum. He is not necessarily the strongest member of the forwards, although hookers are generally big guys. He should be more mobile than his two props. Like the other front-row forwards he should be able to take and receive short passes.

Prop   The props are the 'engine room' of the forward line. They are normally the two strongest players on a team, and that strength is much needed at the scrummage. It is not necessary for a prop to touch the ball in the scrum; his presence alone is often good enough. A weak prop will cost a team dearly.

Lock   The locks play a crucial role. They should be the tallest men in the side. At line-outs they should have the ability to jump and gather the ball or palm it back. Good handling and jumping skills are therefore crucial for the lock forward.

Flanker   Flankers are best described as 'slower three-quarters'. They must be able to break away from the scrummage quickly. The flanker will not be as big as his fellow pack members, and often a flanker will be a converted three-quarter. The flanker has a higher work-rate than the other forwards and is a support for his backs. Therefore, good tackling and handling are essential.

No. 8   Being at the back of the scrum, the No. 8 directs the way the scrum pushes. Taller than the flankers, the No. 8 and flankers are often picked as a 'team' who work well together. In the line-outs the No. 8 plays an important role and, like the locks, should be a good jumper. Being the back-line of the scrum he is also a link between the scrum and his scrum-half and good handling and vision are important. Overall, he should have a sound knowledge of the game and be able to read it well, and take responsibility for directing play at scrums and line-outs.

The backs

Scrum-half   The scrum-half is the focal point of the team. A good scrum-half helps to make a successful team; a bad one can destroy a team. The scrum-half is the link between the forwards and backs and a team can be heartened by his play, not only with a flawless performance but with a spirited one as well. The scrum-half takes a lot of 'stick' from opposing forwards. But he should

Will Carling kicks ahead for England in an international against Canada at the unusual venue of Wembley. This tactic can be most effective when used by fast runners against a line defence.

always have the determination to ride it and continue to motivate his side. Handling is essential for a good scrum-half. He must be able to pick up or gather the ball and pass it quickly, either off the ground or in the air. To add to his all-round ability, the scrum-half needs also to be able to kick (with both feet), feed the scrum accurately, and to be able to tackle from the front, side and rear.

Outside-half *(also known as fly-half or stand-off half)* The principal requirement for a successful outside-half is a sound understanding with his scrum-half. While the scrum-half is the focal point of the team, the outside-half is the player who controls the play. Vision to read the game quickly is essential because he has to make the decision what to do with the ball. Does he start a passing move, or does he kick the ball upfield? He has to decide which will gain his team the best advantage, and which will put the opposition into the most trouble. He must also be able to tackle and also run at the opposition. The outside-half should have the confidence to make the right decisions. He should also have the skill to carry them out.

Centre The centre is involved with play for most of the eighty minutes. He should be a sound tackler as well as being a good runner, handler, passer and kicker. Once he gets the ball he has to decide whether to run at the opposition, pass to an opponent or kick upfield. Being able to take and give passes, particularly with opposing forwards

Catching a high ball

Keep your eyes on the ball.

Make a cradle for the ball.

TECHNIQUE

Receiving the ball from a pass

Meet the ball with the hands then pull the ball into the body.

Clutch the ball to your body.

'gunning' for him, are important attributes.

Winger The winger has a similar role to the centre but he must be the man in the team with the greatest pace. As we have worked our way through the team from the hooker, you will have gathered that the object is to get the ball from the forwards to the scrum-half, and through the backs to either wing man who then, with pace, will hopefully advance upfield to score a try. All the good work of the forwards and other backs will be spoilt if there is a slow or ineffective winger in the team. Running with the ball is the greatest attribute of the winger and he must be able to side-step a defender and pass the ball while travelling at speed.

Full-back The full-back, as part of the backs, plays an attacking and defending role. But his prime function is that of defender. He is the last line of defence and a big responsibility falls on his shoulders. It is plain to see therefore that the full-back must be a confident and capable tackler. Safe hands are also required because the full-

Picking up a loose ball

back often has to collect high balls. His ability to kick is imperative because he may have to kick clear with marauding forwards heading towards him. Because of this kicking skill the full-back is often the player called upon to take place-kicks. At one time the full-back used to spend quite a bit of the game 'hanging around' at the back of the defence waiting for the action to come to him, but these days he is involved more in the play, an essential part of the back division.

The important thing is that all players perform as a team. Admittedly there are two units within one team – the forwards and the backs. But they must work well together. The scrum-half and outside-half are the two key men, because they are the link between the two units. These two, when practising, must

work with the forwards and work out scrummaging and line-out techniques and plans. But after that, they must then work with the backs to see how they are going to generate an attacking move.

That concludes the look at the players. Now we will look at the tasks they will be called upon to perform during a match. Simply, the game can be divided into five categories; catching, passing, running, kicking, and tackling. Then there are the set moves like the line-out and scrummage.

Catching and passing

If you can't catch, then it is most probably worth advising you to put the book down at this stage and take up another sport! If you are still reading, we look next at the

principles of being able to catch the ball, and properly.

By virtue of its shape, the Rugby ball is not the easiest of objects to catch. But, like catching any ball, or anything for that matter, the first principle is **keep your eye on the ball** right up to the time you have it in your possession.

When catching a high ball, make a cradle with your arms for the ball to fall into. Don't put your hands out to catch it solely in the hands. Use the arms as well. Once caught, pull the ball to your chest. You should be standing sideways on to the opposition when making the catch. That way you are ready to set off on a run.

When making a catch from a pass, you have to meet the ball more with your hands. Use them to 'buffer' the ball, and the moment

Pick the ball up in one continuous movement and carry on with the run.

you have made contact, bring the ball close to the chest again.

The ball does not always reach you from a pass or a high ball falling from the air. You will often have to pick up a loose ball off the ground. In that case get down to the ball as low as possible, scoop it up with one hand and continue your forward movement. Don't stop to bend down and pick it up as if you were lacing your shoes . . .

If you are a full-back, many balls that come your way will be bouncing and bobbing all over the place. You must stay calm, and keep your eye on the ball. If you cannot catch the ball while it is in flight, wait

Passing

Keep the ball in front of you.

Look up to see where you are passing to.

*Make the pass with the weight on the right leg
(if passing to the left).*

for it to bounce a couple of times before attempting to gather it.

When **passing** you should hold the ball in front of you before making the pass. This will enable you to get enough movement of the arms to carry out the passing movement. Look up and identify the player you are passing to and make sure the ball is thrown just in front of him (but don't pass the ball forward!). The receiving player should be able to 'run into' the ball. If you pass it directly to the receiver, he will invariably have to stop his run in order to take the ball.

If you are passing to your left then the weight of your body should be on your right foot as you make the pass, and vice versa if you are passing to the right. After letting go of the ball you should bring your non-supporting leg across the supporting one to regain your balance.

The scrum-half should be one of the best

passers on the field, and should be able to get the ball away quickly from the scrummage with a long pass.

The backs should be spread out in a line going away from the scrummage, and to gain maximum advantage should spread out as far away from each other and the scrum as is practicable. For that reason, the scrum-half often has to make a long pass to the first receiving player from the scrum. That is why you will often see him diving full-length as he makes the pass.

The scrum-half will also be required to pick a ball off the ground as it comes out of the scrum, and make a quick pass. He should pick it up and pass it in one continuous movement.

The reverse pass is another pass in the scrum-half's repertoire. It is like the previous pass but made to a player who is running across and behind him. You can now see

RUGBY UNION

A diving pass

Often carried out by the scrum-half.

why we said earlier that the scrum-half must be an all-rounder and have great vision. He must be quick-thinking, and he must also be able to carry out any of the above moves.

One passing rule which you should always remember when playing is: **don't pass to anybody unless they are in a better position than yourself**.

The quick pass

Note how the pass is thrown well in front of the receiving player for him to run on to.

The side-step

Running

When running with the ball the first thing you want to do is make sure you can run with it without dropping it! And, as a general rule, run in a straight line.

Once you have gathered the ball, tuck it in close to your chest and to one side of your body, near your armpit. The other hand should be free to aid the running, and for a hand-off if necessary. You must always be able to get two hands on to the ball ready for the pass.

When running directly at an opponent you should be able to release the ball to a team-mate as the tackle is made. If you cannot get the ball away then you must be confident that your side will retain possession from the maul or ruck . . . if not, don't run straight at an opponent.

A good player will be able to side-step a

defender – one of the most effective ways of beating an opponent. You approach him with the option of beating him on either side but then 'dummy' him into believing you will go one way, but you actually go the opposite way.

When running with the ball timing is crucial, both for the pass and the dummy.

Kicking

You have learned already that there are three types of kick: the place-kick, the drop-kick and the punt. We will now tell you how to perform each kick correctly.

The **place-kick** is used when attempting a kick at goal from a penalty or after a successful try. There are two common forms of place-kick, the straight-kick and the round-the-corner kick.

The first thing to do is make sure the ball is resting in a good position. You should dig a hole in the ground with your heel. It should be big enough to hold the ball, which is placed in the hole on its pointed end. If conditions are very windy, it is advisable to get a team-mate to lie on the ground and hold the ball in position for you.

When adopting the **straight-kick** (see page 62) style you should, after positioning the ball, stand directly over it and in a straight line with the target . . . the goal. The kicking foot should be directly behind the ball and the other foot slightly to the left (or right). You should take approximately six paces backwards (more or less if you prefer).

Once you have reached the point where you will start your run-up, align your eyes from the ball to the target. When you start the run-up, keep the eyes fixed on the ball.

In this sequence the player first goes to his left but then side-steps to the right.

When you arrive at the ball you should be in the same position as you started, i.e. with the kicking foot directly behind the ball and the other foot to one side.

At the moment of starting the back swing of your kicking foot, all your weight should be on the non-kicking foot.

Your head should remain down with your eyes firmly fixed on the ball right up to the last moment. You should make contact with the toe of the boot. Good balance is the key to successful place-kicking.

The **round-the-corner** kick (see page 64) is the style adopted by many kickers in recent years. It is more of a soccer-style kick, in which you make contact with the instep of the boot.

RUGBY UNION

You take up a position at the ball similar to the straight-kick, but your approach to the ball is at an angle, and in an arc. Consequently, the path of the ball will be in an arc, rather than straight.

When you finish your run-up, your weight should again be on the non-kicking foot which, this time, should be more to the left (or right) of the ball, than in the straight-kick. Thereafter, the same principles apply; head well down over the ball, and eyes firmly fixed on it.

With the straight-kick the ball should travel in a straight line. Your target should, therefore, be the middle of the posts. Naturally, wind conditions will dictate where you aim at, and you should make allowances for such conditions.

Place-kicking is an art. To become successful you have to practise. Fortunately, you can practise kicking on your own. When you first start, you should try easy kicks directly under the posts, then start moving the ball backwards towards the halfway line, and then try moving to both sides.

Balance is also important when attempting a **drop-kick** (see page 66). The ball should be held in both hands, one on either side, and allowed to drop to the ground; don't throw the ball up in the air first. At the same time the leg is swung back, and the kick is carried out at the moment the ball hits the ground. A good follow through is imperative.

Like the place-kick, you can have a round-the-corner drop-kick, which the novice will find easier. However, the straight kick is more effective and you are well advised to try and develop this type of kick right from the start. If you are successful with it, you will reap the benefits when you get into a match.

The straight place-kick

TECHNIQUE

The principles for the **punt** (see page 67) are the same as the drop-kick. Timing and balance are the key. This time, the ball is kicked before it hits the ground.

You want to practise punting with both feet because you will often be put under pressure when punting and there will often not be time to get in a position to change feet. With punting, concentrate on accuracy . . . get the ball to go in the direction you want it to.

The main object of the punt is to find touch; if you don't you will very likely give possession to the opposing team. If you are successful in finding touch then you have a 50-50 chance of retaining possession from the line-out.

Tackling

There are four basic types of tackle: head-on tackle, side-on tackle, smother tackle and the tackle from behind. Good timing is the key to successful tackling. Always remember: if you are unsuccessful with your tackle then you will have lost your team a player . . . you will be left sprawling on the ground! So make sure your tackling is positive.

When making a **head-on tackle** (see page 68) you should approach the opponent at a slight angle. The target area is just above his waist.

You should aim for this area with your shoulder and wrap your arms around his body. Invariably, the opponent's momentum will carry him over the top of the tackler.

The **side-on tackle** (see page 69) is made with the shoulder hitting the target area around the attacker's thigh. The arms should be wrapped around his legs. There is a good chance that, as the tackler, you will be on top of your opponent after the tackle and thus be in a position to play the ball first after it has been released.

The round-the-corner place-kick

Note how the approach to the ball differs from the straight kick.

Scrum-half Gareth Edwards played 53 consecutive games for Wales between 1967 and 1978, during which time they won the international championship seven times.

RUGBY UNION

Drop-kick

This sequence shows the round-the-corner drop-kick.

TECHNIQUE

The left-footed punt

Note the balance at the moment of the kick and the follow-through.

RUGBY UNION

Head-on tackle

TECHNIQUE

Side-on tackle

Note how, in both types of tackle, the shoulder connects with the target area.

RUGBY UNION

Tackle from behind

TECHNIQUE

Smother tackle

When **tackling from behind** the target area is the same as for the side-on tackle, but keep your head well to one side and away from the attacker's legs. The tackle from behind has a greater element of surprise to it and that, together with the wrapping of the arms around the legs, and natural momentum, will bring the man down.

The **smother tackle** is designed to prevent your opponent making a pass as he is tackled. With the other types of tackle, it could be possible for the attacker to make a pass as you tackle. The smother tackle is designed to prevent that. It is called a smother tackle because you smother your opponent's arms. The tackle is best made

Line-out, throwing the ball in

See how the thrower looks to the players in the line . . .

. . . lines up the ball . . .

from the side, and after wrapping your arms around his, you should push forward. Momentum will take him to the ground and prevent a pass.

All tackles are made by driving into the tackle off one leg, and use of the shoulder is important. Tackling is achieved not only with the hands. Most players prefer to tackle using the right shoulder but you are strongly advised to practise tackling with both shoulders. It will give you more flexibility when you get onto the field.

Line-out

At the line-out a good team will have a carefully worked-out plan. The player throwing in the ball will have given some sort of signal indicating to which part of the line he is throwing the ball, thus giving his players advance warning.

If you throw the ball in, you should hold the ball with both hands and near to the end. If you are throwing right-handed, your left leg should be forward with your weight

... prepares to throw. When you do it, make sure it goes in straight.

on it. Keep your eyes on your target man, and pull your throwing arm back and gently release the ball.

The target man, generally the No. 8 or a lock, should anticipate the throw and make sure he jumps to gather, or palm the ball before his opposite number can get to it. When the target man has got the ball it is important for the other players in the line-out to support him, otherwise the opposing forwards will be on him like the proverbial 'ton of bricks'.

If the target man catches the ball, his fellow forwards should assist him by blocking, thus giving him the freedom to get the ball out to his scrum-half.

Palming the ball out of the line-out is often done from the centre or end of the line. It is not just a case of jumping and 'slapping' the ball out. But it should be carefully directed, either with one or two hands, to your scrum-half. Always make sure you know where your scrum-half is at the line-out. He is the man you are trying to get the ball to.

RUGBY UNION

Support at the line-out

Note how the other forwards protect the man with the ball . . .

. . . who has no problem getting it back to his scrum-half.

Scrummage

We have already seen how and when a scrummage is formed. Let us look at the best ways of getting the maximum benefit from a scrummage.

Always make sure you are tightly bound around the next man. This will give a solid and effective scrum and will help as you push forward against the opposing forwards; it will also help you absorb any pressure they may put on you.

All players in the scrum should pack down low and their feet should be a comfortable distance apart. The back should be straight and the knees bent. The head should be in such a position that the player can get up as

soon as the ball comes out of the scrummage.

If the opposing side has the put-in, you can still play an important part in the outcome of the scrum. Make life tough for the opposing side by pushing against them or, alternatively, wheeling the scrum, i.e. turning it around.

We saw earlier that there are many different ways (or channels) the ball can come out of the scrum. Once the hooker has decided which one will be adopted, it doesn't mean the players not involved can sit back and rest . . . *all* players have an important role. The scrum is a team effort and all players should work together as one unit.

Palming the ball from the line-out

Be positive, and palm with either one or two hands. Make sure you direct the ball to your scrum-half.

Throughout the *Play the Game* series we have stressed the need to practise. This book cannot make you a great player, that is up to you. And the only way to become great is to practise, and practise, and practise. Hopefully, the more you practise the more you will enjoy the game.

USEFUL
ADDRESSES

Australian Rugby Football Union
Rugby Union House
Crane Place
Sydney
New South Wales, 27777
Australia

French Rugby Federation
(Fédération Française de Rugby)
7 Cité d'Antin
75009 Paris
France

Irish Rugby Football Union
62 Lansdowne Road
Dublin 4
Republic of Ireland

New Zealand Rugby Football Union
Huddart Parker Building
Post Office Square
PO Box 2172
Wellington
New Zealand

Rugby Football Union
Twickenham
Middlesex TW1 1DZ
England

Scottish Rugby Football Union
Murrayfield
Edinburgh 12
Scotland

South African Rugby Board
Boundary Road
Newlands 7700
South Africa

Welsh Rugby Football Union
National Stadium
Cardiff
Wales

RULES CLINIC
INDEX

Many new countries are pressing for entry into higher ranks of international rugby and the 1991 World Cup saw Canada and Western Samoa perform particularly well. The Fijians have long delightful crowds around the world with their strong forward play and entertaining running.

INDEX